D1716093

Form and Function

Why should a gold-chased dress sword be considered more worthy of a place in a museum than a skillfully made, perfectly balanced, kitchen knife? Why is the former considered more "beautiful" than the knife? Both treasure and tool are artifacts; each has its own qualities and neither deserves neglect. Yet everyday objects are never valued as highly as things made for visual appeal, to display artistry, technical virtuosity, copious embellishment, or bright and rare materials—pretty, precious, shiny things.

When exposure to shoddy, mass-produced, ill-designed objects reaches some critical point, then people come to appreciate the forms and qualities of common things crafted and shaped through generations of human experience. These books focus upon objects hitherto either taken for granted or disregarded as commonplace.

Each book in the series represents a select unity of functional forms; each object is informed with the beauty born from function. The photographs choreograph the objects and enhance them without artifice. Every object speaks for itself yet relates intimately to other objects of the same type.

Japanese objects form the basis for this series because they are of high craftsmanship and are still made in quantity. One of the principles of the series is availability. Although a few objects are antiques and relatively difficult to find without sustained effort, most are made now and can be purchased from the shops, makers, and sources listed in the back of the books.

The aim of this series is to make the reader approach practical objects as a fresh experience and know the profound satisfaction to be had from owning and frequently using well-crafted things, the successful marriage of form and function.

Form & Function titles

1 Japanese Brushes
2 Japanese Knives
3 Japanese Spoons and Ladles

In preparation

4 Japanese Teapots
5 Japanese Boxes
6 Japanese Bamboo Baskets

Contents

庖丁

Form
and
Function
series

JAPANESE KNIVES

Introduction by Yoshio Akioka
Photographs by Masao Usui

Kodansha International
Tokyo, New York and San Francisco

distributed
in the United States
by Kodansha International/USA Ltd.,
through Harper & Row, Publishers, Inc.,
10 East 53rd Street, New York, New York 10022.

published
by Kodansha International Ltd.,
2−12−21 Otowa, Bunkyo-ku, Tokyo 112
and Kodansha International/USA Ltd.,
10 East 53rd Street, New York, New York 10022
and 44 Montgomery Street, San Francisco, California 94104.

first edition, 1979

20Mar'80

LCC 78−71255
ISBN 0−87011−371−2
JBC 2372−787325−2361

Japanese Knives

Yoshio Akioka

It is a surprising fact that, in the highly industrialized Japan of today, there are still many smiths in the nation's capital who hand-fashion various types of cutlery. In their workshops located in the narrow canyons between high-rise buildings, these smiths make blade tools—knives, chisels, planes, and drawshaves—on order from craftsmen, carpenters, and furniture makers living in the metropolis. Some smiths specialize in making fine scissors by hand for gardening or flower arranging; others make high-quality kitchen knives (*hōchō*) for professional chefs. All these metalworkers use techniques essentially unchanged for the past century.

Carpenters and artisans who take pride in their work are meticulous about the quality of the tools they use. They prefer to order tools from neighborhood blacksmiths rather than buy ready-made ones mass-produced in factories; they always want their tools to be the best. Tokyo is probably the only capital of an advanced, industrialized nation in which skilled smiths still produce tools by hand, supported by the orders of artisans nearby who themselves employ traditional skills in their work.

There are many such smiths in other Japanese towns and cities as well. In Kyoto a rather large number of skilled smiths produce the various types of Kyoto cutlery. They make, for instance, a special knife that is essential for preparing *hamo*, an eel favored in Kyoto cuisine. The *hamo* has a great number of tiny bones, making it difficult to prepare without the proper tools. The Kyoto knife for preparing *unagi*, another kind of eel, is completely different in shape from the *unagi* knife used in Tokyo for the same purpose (photo, p. 37). Since Kyoto is one of the centers of Japanese haute cuisine, and since the blades made in that city are ordered by chefs specializing in Kyoto cooking, there is little doubt that the characteristic knives of this ancient city will continue to be made for a long time.

Another example is the town of Hitoyoshi in Kyushu, which does not have a large population but which was once a castle town and still boasts its own characteristic culture. Today three craftsmen remain who make the special Hitoyoshi knife. The town, in the mountains far from the ocean, has

7

a lovely river where the residents have long caught fish for food. The Hitoyoshi kitchen knife is designed to combine two seemingly incompatible functions—preparation of both fish and vegetables. Knives for these two uses usually have very different shapes and blades. People of Hitoyoshi use only the knives made by the three blacksmiths in the town, even though mass-produced, stainless steel knives made in distant factories are available at cheaper prices, and they proudly claim that Hitoyoshi cooking is best prepared using local cutlery.

The fine-quality chisels, utility knives, and kitchen knives produced today in places like Tokyo, Kyoto, and Hitoyoshi are not of stainless steel; they are made by layering iron and steel in a technique unique to Japan. A cross-section of the blade of a household kitchen knife shows a core of steel sandwiched between layers or beneath one layer of soft iron. Only a thin line of hard steel is exposed—the cutting edge. Japanese cutlery is fashioned in this way because it makes a blade easier to sharpen, to shape, and to use as a precision instrument.

Most fine-quality Japanese kitchen blades are made for special, professional uses. Knives used by professional chefs are heavier and balanced differently from the ordinary household blade. A professional cook lets the weight of his knife work for him, thus saving a great deal of energy. A Japanese chef uses the proper tool for a given job—he does not cut meat with a knife designed for fish, nor will he use a fish knife for cutting vegetables. This results in an enormous variety of knives. The number for fish alone is amazing—there are special knives for horse mackeral, for squid, for tuna, for delicate slices of raw fish (*sashimi*), and for various kinds of *sushi*, to mention but a few. The making of buckwheat noodles (*soba*) also involves a special knife (p. 44). Even in cases where the shapes of different knives do not vary greatly, the size, weight, and thickness are precisely matched to the preparation of a certain food, and there are also many different cutting-edge angles and shapes. Besides the vocabulary of knife forms made for Japanese cuisine, Japanese knives for Western cooking, also, are surpassed by none in the world.

Quality knives cannot be mass-produced. They must be made by hand, one blade at a time, according to the old techniques. In Japan, despite the race toward mass-production and standardization, the craftsman's strong, almost imperative sense that a tool must match the job is still very much alive.

庖　丁

秋 岡 芳 夫

　驚いたことに、極度に工業化の進んだ国日本の首都東京に、手作りでいろいろな刃物を作る鍛冶たちが多勢住んでいる。

　彼らは高層ビルのつくる谷間に小さな工房風の仕事場を構えて、同じく東京に住んでいる工芸家や大工や建具屋の要求に応じてノミ・彫刻刃・鉋を作っている。庭師用や華道用の鋏を一丁一丁ていねいに手作りしている鍛冶もいる。調理師用の高級庖丁を作る鍛冶もいて、どの鍛冶もみな、そろって百年前とさほど変わらない工法で木工具や鋏や庖丁を作っている。

　東京に手作りの鍛冶が多勢住んでいるのは、東京に工芸家や大工が彫刻家が多勢住んでいて伝統工具の需要が多いからである。彫刻家・工芸家そして仕事熱心な大工は道具（刃物）にことのほかうるさくて、仲間よりも一層上等の道具を持とうとする。近代工場で量産した既成品の刃物よりも近所に住んでいる鍛冶に注文で作らせた刃物の方を好んで使う。

　先進国の首都で、この東京のように伝統的な手道具を愛用している多勢の工芸家や大工が、手作りの鍛冶と同居している街はおそらく例を見ないことだと思う。

　手作りの刃物鍛冶が街に住みついている例は、日本でなら随所で見ることができる。

　たとえば京都だが、京都には腕のいい庖丁鍛冶が多勢いて、いろいろな型の京風の庖丁を作っている。

　京都の人たちははもという魚が好物だが、このはもは小さな骨が多くて料理の難しい魚である。はも専用の庖丁でないとうまく料理することができない。また京都では、うなぎを料理するのに東京のとは全く違う形をした庖丁を使う。こうした京都独特の調理法に合わせたいろいろな調理庖丁を、京の刃物鍛冶たちは調理人からあれこれと注文をつけてもらいながら作りつづけている。こうした風土性豊かな庖丁類はこれから先も京都で長く作りつづけられるに違いない。

　九州の人吉という町の人口は、さほど多くはないがかつては城下町として独特の文化を誇っていたところである。この町には今も三軒、人吉型という独特の庖丁を作っている鍛冶が残っている。人吉という町は海からは遠く離れていて、四方を山に囲まれている。美しい川が町の中を流れていて、ここの人たちは川魚をさかんに食べて暮してきた。そのためにここ人吉の家庭用の庖丁は、一丁で魚も野菜も料理できるという魚菜兼用の形をしている。人吉の人たちは町に一緒に住んでいる三人の鍛冶の作る庖丁しか使わない。遠くの工場で量産しているステンレスの庖丁は、たとえその方が安くとも、使いにくいと言って使わない。人吉の家庭料理は人吉の庖丁で作った方がうまい。そう人吉の人たちは自慢する。

ところで、現在東京や京都や人吉で作っている刃物にはステンレス鋼は使われていない。ノミも小刀も庖丁も全鋼製ではなくて、鉄と鋼を積層にした日本独特の作り方で作ってある。

　たとえば家庭用の庖丁の刃の断層を見ると芯の鋼を両側から軟らかな鉄が挟んでいて、まるでサンドイッチのようである。挟まれた鋼はほんの少し刃先にのぞいていて、刃物全体は鈍い色をした鉄で作られている。調理師の使う庖丁はぶ厚い鉄と薄い鋼の二層構造になっている。

　日本の刃物がその大部分を軟らかな鉄で作られ、刃先にだけ鋼がのぞくような構造になっているのは、研ぎやすいからである。

　日本の庖丁は、家庭用の庖丁を除いたらその大半が専用の庖丁である。魚用の庖丁で肉を切るようなことは日本の調理師はしない。魚用の庖丁で野菜を刻むこともまたない。

　魚用の庖丁だけでもびっくりする程の種類がある。あじ専用の庖丁もある。先に書いたようにうなぎやはも専用の庖丁もある。刺身専用の庖丁もある。

　またすし専用の庖丁やそば専用の庖丁もあって日本の庖丁はバラエティに富んでいる。形にさほどの違いは見られないが、大きさや刃物の厚みや目方が、微妙に調理するものに合わせて変えてある。刃の研ぎ角もまたさまざまである。

　こうした多品種の刃物群は大工場では作りたがらない。一丁一丁、昔ながらの工法で作らないと作れない。

　東京や京都や人吉や、人吉に代表される各地の町で、その土地独特の庖丁を作っているのはまた、土地土地で食べ物が違うからである。食べ物が変ればそれに合わせて庖丁も変える。これが日本の伝統なのである。

KNIVES

13

24

27

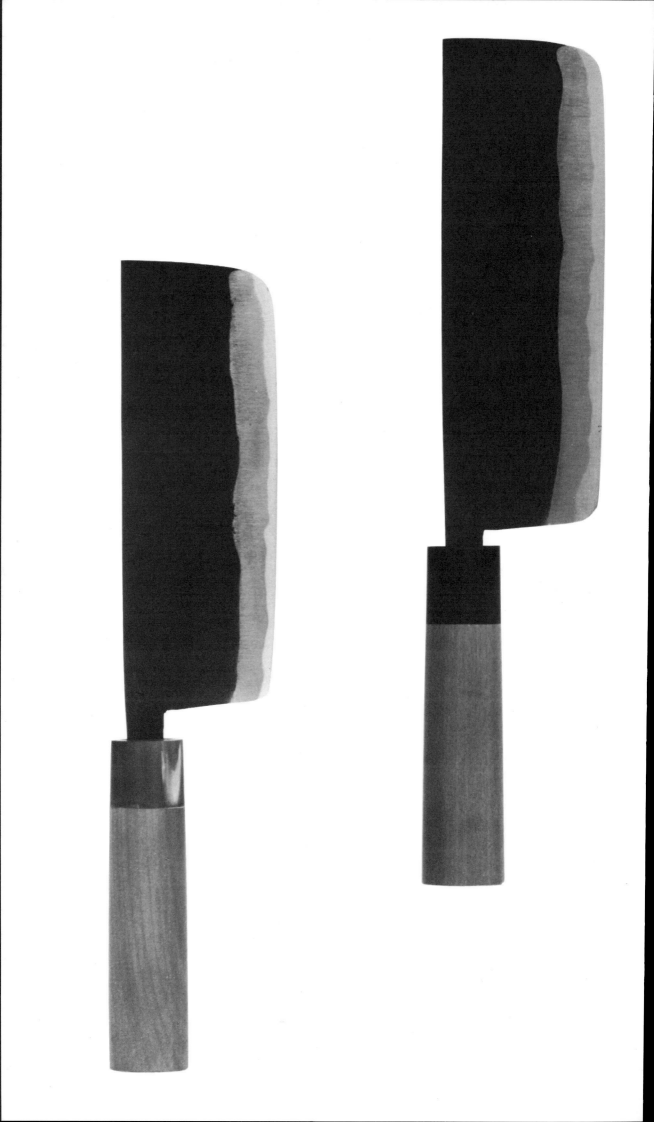

32

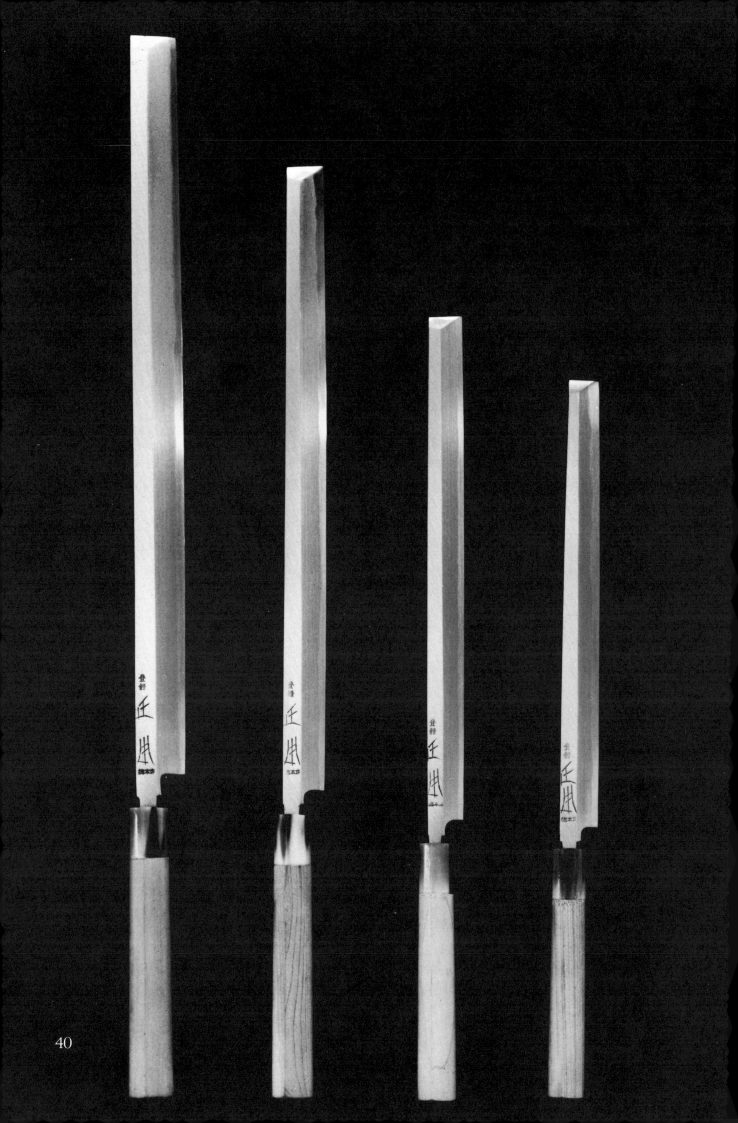

40

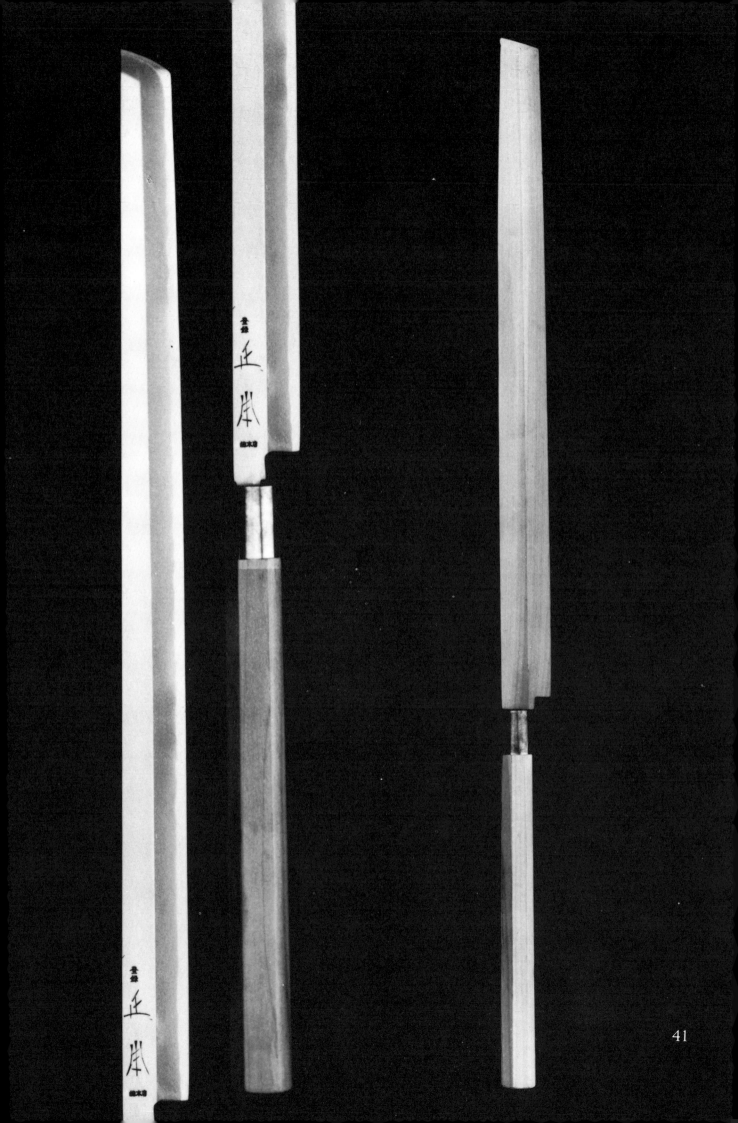

41

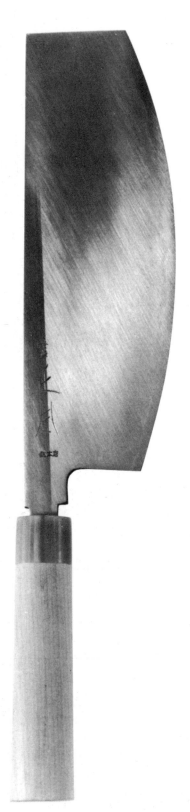

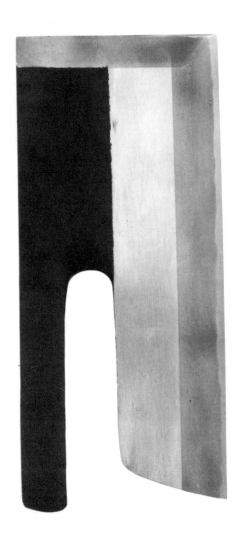

46

47

51

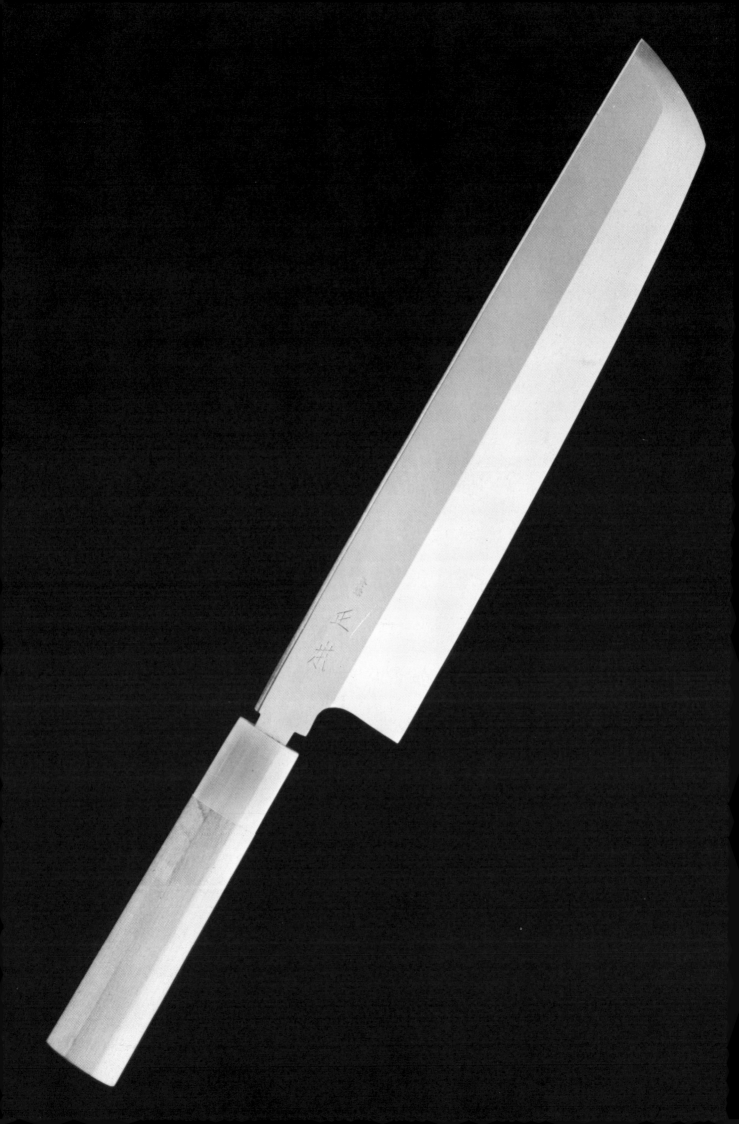

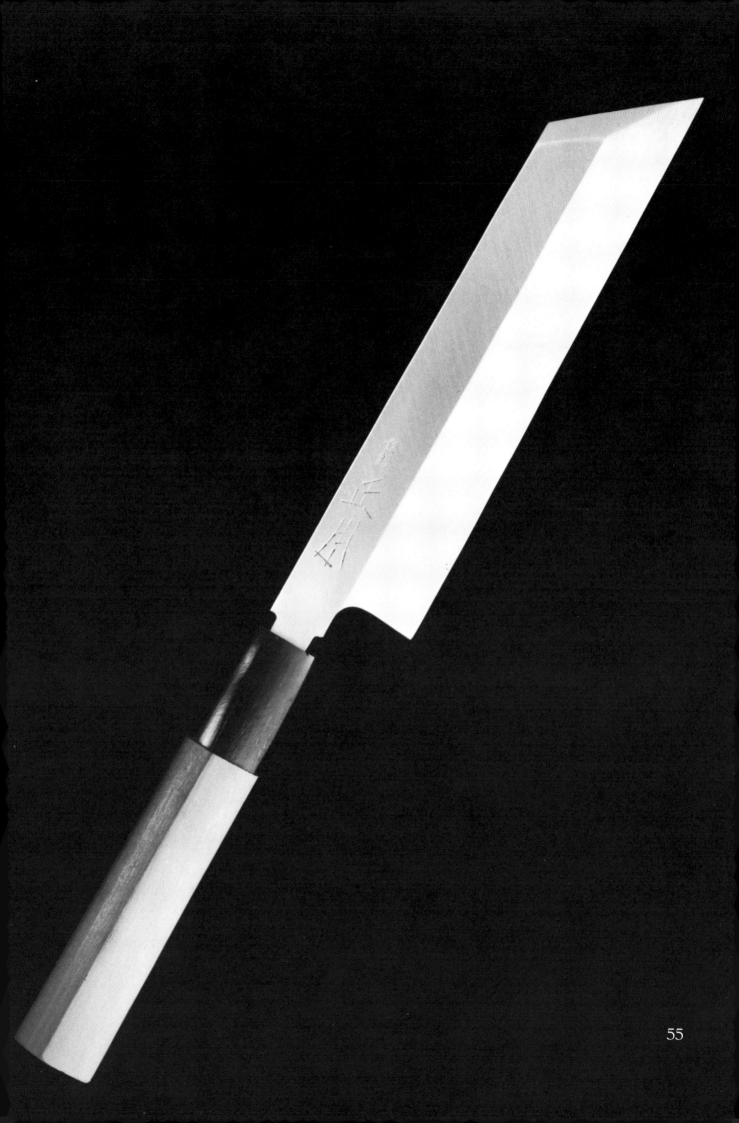

61

63

64

Captions

The reason why the knives (*hōchō*) of only one maker are reproduced here is because standard shapes made by commercial smiths do not vary greatly and, generally, the same types of knives are made by all the major companies.

The knives on pages 45 to 55 duplicate many of the knife types on the preceding pages. This short section shows the highest-quality knives, those known as *hon-yaki*, as compared to *hon-gasumi*, ordinary Japanese knives. The *hon-yaki* knife blade is made entirely of steel, while the *hon-gasumi* blade resembles an open-faced sandwich, with thin steel forming the cutting edge and a thicker layer of iron over it, as described in the introduction. The tangs of all blades must be of iron, since steel is too brittle for this use. The *hon-yaki* blades cost hundreds of dollars each and are used by professional cooks. They cut better and last longer than less expensive knives.

Most Japanese knife types are sharpened on one side (usually the right) only, but a few types, such as the *nakiri-bōchō* (vegetable knife), for household use are sharpened on both sides. A blade sharpened on one side only generally cuts much better, faster, and cleaner than a blade sharpened on both sides.

The lengths given below refer to blades only and do not include the handles.

p. 13. *Katsuo-bushi* knives; (l.) 39 cm. These knives are used to cut out the flesh of the bonito (*katsuo*), which is dried (*katsuo-bushi*) and eventually shaved for use in making soup stock. The work is specialized, but these knives seem to be generalized versions of the highly developed forms that appear in this book, hence their inclusion at the beginning. The handles are of pine with the bark intact; this allows a firm grip in this greasy work.

p. 14. Various Japanese knives (identified in captions below).

p. 15. Kitchen knife set; (l.) 33.5 cm. Kitchen knives traditionally were sold in sets of three, without handles and un-sharpened (the right-hand knife showing the unsharpened edge is a smaller version of the one in the center). It was the user's responsibility to sharpen and shape the edge and make a handle to fit his or her own hand and work habits. All Japanese edged tools were once sold unsharpened and without handles.

p. 16. Standard *deba-bōchō* (fish knives); (l.) length 34 cm., thickness 9 mm. The knife on the right was once the same size as the one on the left (as can be seen by comparing thicknesses) but years of extensive use and sharpening have greatly reduced the size and changed the shape. The handle of the older knife has been modified for some special purpose.

p. 17.   Regional knife forms; (l.) 32 cm. From left, vegetable knife, Kumamoto Pref.; vegetable knife, Kōchi Pref.; vegetable-fish knife (see introduction, p. 7), Hitoyoshi, Kumamoto Pref.; fish knife, Kōchi Pref. The first three are classified as *nakiri-bōchō*, the last as a *deba-bōchō*, but in these regional variations, the two forms merge one into another.

pp. 18, 19.   Standard *deba-bōchō* (fish knives); (from l.) 30–12 cm. in 3-cm. decrements, 10.5, 7.5 cm. The larger the fish, the larger the knife that is used, but often the smallest sizes of this type are used as general utility knives in Japanese household kitchens. Various forms of *deba-bōchō* follow.

p. 20.   *Oroshi deba-bōchō*; (from l.) 24, 22.5, 21 cm. These are for finer cutting of fish than the standard *deba-bōchō*.

p. 21.   *Ai deba-bōchō*; (from l.) 24, 15, 18, 21 cm. This form has exactly the same use as the *oroshi deba* in the preceding photograph, but there is no notch on the tang. Choice of knife is a matter of personal preference.

p. 22.   *Kuro-uchi deba-bōchō*; (from l.) 30, 27, 24, 21, 18 cm. The regular *deba-bōchō* is used by cooks, but these knives are used by fishmongers. The black knives are heavier than the polished blades.

p. 23.   *Sake-kiri deba-bōchō*; (from l.) 30, 27, 24 cm. This is used only for salmon and is thinner and lighter than the *kuro-uchi deba-bōchō* in the previous photograph.

pp. 24, 25.   *Kiri-tsuki hōchō*; (from l., each page) 33, 30, 27 cm. These knives combine the functions of the "willow leaf"

sashimi slicer, *nakiri-bōchō* (vegetable knife), and *deba-bōchō* (fish knife). On page 25, only the right side of the blade is sharpened; on page 24, both sides are sharpened.

pp. 26, 27.   *Regional nakiri-bōchō* (vegetable knife) forms; (l, p. 26) 30.5 cm. From left, Seki, Gifu Pref.; Kōchi Pref.; Kōchi Pref.; Yufuin-chō, Ōita Pref.; Tokyo; Aizu, Fukushima Pref. The second knife from Kōchi (rt., p. 26) shows the style of western (Kansai area) Japan; the others are all in the eastern (Kantō) style (see also photo, p. 30). The Tokyo blade is well worn, and the Aizu blade is sharpened on the right side only. There are many other regional variations, but this is a spot sampling of representative types from the northern, central, and southern parts of the country. Various vegetable knife styles follow.

pp. 28, 29.   *Nakiri-bōchō*; (from l., each page) 15, 16.5 cm. These are identified in the maker's catalogue as being vegetable knives with water buffalo horn sleeves. They are for household rather than professional use; the black blade is heavier than the polished. The maker calls household-use vegetable knives *nakiri-bōchō*; vegetable knives for professional chefs are *usu-ba*.

p. 30.   Eastern style *usu-ba*; (from l.) 27, 22.5, 19.5, 16.5 cm. The square corner of the blade nearest the handle and the overall square shape defines the eastern style, i.e., the knife style of the Kantō (Tokyo) area and northwards. This is the widest of the vegetable knives. The small size is used to peel; the middle size is used to cut fine, continuous shavings; the large size is for chopping.

p. 31. "Sickle" style (*kama-gata*) *usu-ba*; (from l.) 24, 21, 18, 15 cm. This curved blade is the Kansai, or western, style of vegetable knife. The use is the same as the other vegetable knives (*usu-ba*) mentioned here; for all these knives, personal preference determines which will be used.

p. 32. "Square" (*kaku-gata*) *usu-ba*; (from l.) 24, 21 cm. This vegetable knife with right-angled blade corners has the same use as the vegetable knives already mentioned.

p. 33. "Rhomboid" (*hishi-gata*) *usu-ba*; (from l.) 24, 21 cm. This is another variety of knife for cutting vegetables.

p. 34. *Hamo* eel knives (*hamo hone-kiri hōchō*); (from l.) 33, 30, 27 cm. Anyone who has tried to eat a poorly cut and trimmed *hamo* eel and has encountered the endless tiny bones knows how important the proper knife and skill are in the preparation of this fish. The bones cannot be eliminated, but the diner will not notice them in a properly prepared *hamo*.

p. 35. Loach knives (*dojō-saki hōchō*); (from l.) 18, 15, 12 cm. The large knife on the left is for *anago* eels, the smaller ones are for loach.

p. 36. Tokyo style *unagi* eel knives (*unagi-saki hōchō*); (from l.) 30, 27, 24, 21 cm. The three types of eel mentioned here are all quite different in structure and flavor; naturally, the cuisines vary and so do the knives used to prepare the eels.

p. 37. Regional *unagi* eel knife forms; (from l.) 26, 22.5, 21 cm. From left, Nagoya, Kyoto, Osaka. The startling differences in regional *unagi* knife forms is due to local differences in *unagi* cuisine.

p. 38. "Willow leaf" *sashimi* knives (*yanagi-ba sashimi bōchō*); (from l.) 39 to 18 cm. in 3-cm. decrements. This type of knife for slicing fish is from the Kansai (Osaka-Kyoto; i.e., western) area and is more versatile than the *tako-biki* type on page 40 (q.v.).

p. 39. Blowfish *sashimi* knives (*fugu-biki sasaimi bōchō*); (from l.) 36, 30, 24 cm. This resembles the "willow leaf" knife in the previous photograph, but this blade is thinner and the cutting edge straighter.

p. 40. *Tako-biki sashimi* knives; (from l.) 39, 33, 27, 24 cm. This is the Kantō (Tokyo, i.e., eastern) area style of *sashimi* knife. Its blade is thinner than the "willow leaf" blade and it can only be used to slice. Before World War II, this type comprised 90 percent of the *sashimi* knives. Today, because of the greater versatility of the "willow leaf" type, only 30 percent of the *sashimi* knives in use are of the *tako-biki* style.

p. 41. Tuna knife (l.) and sheath; 60 cm. This knife is the length of a sword—the tuna is large, and so is the knife that is made to cut it.

p. 42. *Sushi* cutters; (from l.) 24, 22.5, 21 cm. Osaka style *sushi* is made by putting thin slices of fish over a loaf of rice, which is then cut into individual servings, as compared to the usual *sushi*, in which the rice for each serving is shaped by hand and the fish then laid on. This knife type is used to cut the large Osaka *sushi* loaves.

p. 43. Chinese cleavers; (from l.) 22, 23, 21 cm. Thickness, not size, determines the use of the Chinese cleaver. Thin blades are for vegetables and meat: medium, for vege-

71

tables and fish; thick, for chopping meat with bones.

p. 44. Noodle cutters; (bottom, l., rt.) 24, 30, 33 cm. The speed with which a professional noodle maker can use these knives to cut through the many layers of thin dough has to be seen to be believed.

p. 45. Variety of hon-yaki knives (see introduction to captions and captions below).

p. 46. (Hon-yaki) tako-biki sashimi knives (from l.) 36, 33, 30, 27, 24 cm.

p. 47. (Hon-yaki) tako-biki sashimi knives with wide blades and rounded tips; (from rt.) 36, 33, 31.5, 30 cm.

pp. 48, 49. (Hon-yaki) "willow leaf" sashimi knives; (from l.) 39–24 cm. in 3-cm. decrements.

p. 49 right. (Hon-yaki) blowfish sashimi knife; 33 cm.

p. 50. (Hon-yaki) "eastern" style usu-ba (vegetable knife); 21 cm.

p. 51. (Hon-yaki) "sickle" style usu-ba (vegetable knife); (from l.) 24, 22.5, 21 cm.

p. 52. (Hon-yaki) "square" usu-ba (vegetable knife); (from l.) 24, 22.5, 21 cm.

p. 53. (Hon-yaki) kiri-tsuki hōchō; both 30 cm. The knife on the left is sharpened on both sides of the blade; that on the right, on the right side only.

p. 54. (Hon-yaki) hamo eel knife; 30 cm.

p. 55. (Hon-yaki) "rhomboid" usu-ba; 18

cm. This small vegetable knife is for making flowers and decorative displays out of various vegetables.

p. 56. Ceremonial knife and chopsticks; 30 cm. These are used for special ceremonies at which professional cooks officiate.

p. 57. "Masamoto," the name of the maker of most of the knives in this book. The name itself is chiseled by hand into each blade, but stamps are used for accompanying words.

pp. 58, 59. Various Western kitchen knives (identified in captions below). Both handles and shapes of Western knives differ greatly from their Japanese counterparts, but, the maker states, his Western knives (reproduced here) have been somewhat adapted and changed from the original forms to meet the needs of Japanese cooks. A luxurious and practical touch is the use of rosewood for many knife handles.

p. 60. Western deba-bōchō (kitchen knives?) with guards; (from top) 30, 27, 24 21 cm. Despite the term deba-bōchō, these are not fish knives. The top two are professional cook's knives for vegetables and meat, respectively, and the bottom two are for general household use.

p. 61. Suji-biki (tendon removing) knives; (from l.) 30, 27, 24 cm. The maker states that this knife, which is used to remove tendons, ligaments, fat, and tough tissues from meat, has no counterpart in the West.

pp. 62, 63. Gyūtō (general kitchen) knives with rosewood handles; (from l.) 39–27 cm. in 3-cm. decrements, 25.5, 24,

21, 18, 17 cm. The three on the right are for general household use; the next three are for meat; the four on the left are for vegetables.

p. 64. Paring knives with guards and rosewood handles; (from l.) 15, 13.5, 12 cm. These are all-purpose household knives.

p. 65. Boning knives; (from l.) 18, 15, 13.5 cm. The two small knives are for beef, pork, etc., while the large knife is for boning chicken.

p. 66. Boneless ham slicers; (from l.) 42, 39, 36, 33 cm. These seem to be carving knives for meat; they are only used in fancy restaurants and hotels.

p. 67. Cake and bread knives; (from l.) 42, 39, 36, 33, 30 cm.

p. 68. From left, frozen food knife, meat chopper, smoked salmon slicer; 30, 18, 24 cm. The knife for frozen food should be best termed a hacker rather than a cutter; it is made to handle large hunks of frozen food. The salmon slicer is also practical for roast beef, turkey, etc.

写真解説

13ページ
鰹節作りが使う庖丁
脂で滑らないように柄を皮つきの松の枝で作ってある。
左の庖丁　39.0㎝（全長）

14ページ
和庖丁各種

15ページ
日本独特の庖丁の売り方
刃もつけず、柄もすげずに、こんな姿で庖丁を売ることがしばしばある。高級な庖丁の売買に多いケースだ。使用者が好みの刃角に研ぎ、好みの柄をすげて使う。
左の庖丁　33.5㎝（全長）

16ページ
出刃庖丁
これらは、板前が魚料理に使う標準的な出刃庖丁で、左が新しいもの。右が使いこんだもの。研ぎながら、刃の形を使いやすいように変えてゆく。柄も手と仕事に合わせて、削りながら使う。背巾の厚さから、この二本の出刃は同じ大きさのものだったことがわかる。
左の庖丁　34.0㎝（全長）
刃の厚み　9㎜

17ページ
各地方の庖丁
左から熊本の菜切庖丁、高知の菜切庖丁、熊本人吉の菜切庖丁、高知の魚用庖丁。
左の庖丁　32.2㎝（全長）

18・19ページ
出刃庖丁
大きい出刃庖丁は大きい魚に、小さい出刃庖丁は小さい魚に使われる。
左より30.0㎝　27.0㎝　24.0㎝　21.0㎝
18.0㎝　15.0㎝　12.0㎝　10.5㎝　7.5㎝

20ページ
おろし出刃庖丁
普通の出刃より刃の巾がやや狭く、薄くできており魚をおろしたり、皮をひいたりするのに使う。
左より24.0㎝　22.5㎝　21.0㎝

21ページ
相出刃庖丁
おろし出刃庖丁と同じように使われる。
左より24.0㎝　15.0㎝　18.0㎝　21.0㎝

22ページ
黒打出刃庖丁
魚屋で使われる庖丁で磨きをかけていない。概して黒打の庖丁は、総磨きのものよりも重い。
左より30.0㎝　27.0㎝　24.0㎝　21.0㎝　18.0㎝

23ページ
鮭切黒打出刃庖丁
鮭を切るのに使われる。
左より30.0㎝　27.0㎝　24.0㎝

24ページ
切付庖丁（片刃）
野菜にも魚にも使われる庖丁で、柳刃、出刃、

薄刃の三種の庖丁の役割を果す。俗に無精庖丁ともよばれている。
左より33.0cm　30.0cm　27.0cm

25ページ
切付庖丁（諸刃）
片刃庖丁の方が切れ味がよく、専門の調理師は、普通、片刃庖丁を使う。
左より33.0cm　30.0cm　27.0cm

26・27ページ
各地方の庖丁
左から大分県湯布院町の菜切庖丁、東京の使いこんだ菜切庖丁、会津の片刃の菜切庖丁、岐阜県関の西型菜切庖丁、高知の西型菜切庖丁、高知の東型菜切庖丁。
左端の庖丁　30.5cm（全長）

28・29ページ
菜切庖丁
家庭でごく普通に使われる野菜用の庖丁。専門の調理師はこの種の菜切庖丁は使わない。
左より15.0cm　16.5cm　15.0cm　16.5cm

30ページ
東型薄刃庖丁
専門の調理師が使う野菜用の庖丁。この形のものは東型とよばれ、静岡以北で使われている。主として大型のものは野菜きざみに、中型のものは桂むきに、小型のものは皮むきに使われる。
左より27.0cm　22.5cm　19.5cm　16.5cm

31ページ
鎌型薄刃庖丁
関西型の野菜用の庖丁。
左より24.0cm　21.0cm　18.0cm　15.0cm

32・33ページ
角型薄刃庖丁（32ページ）**菱型薄刃庖丁**（33ページ）
専門の調理師が好んで使う野菜用の庖丁。
左より24.0cm　21.0cm　24.0cm　21.0cm

34ページ
鱧切り
鱧の骨切りに使われる鱧専用の庖丁。
左より33.0cm　30.0cm　27.0cm

35ページ
穴子さきと鱚さき
左が穴子さき、右の二つが鱚さき。柄は、手の中におさまるように小さくできている。
左より18.0cm　15.0cm　12.0cm

36ページ
鰻さき
穴子さきや鱚さきと同型だが、それらより大型である。これは東京の鰻さき。
左より30.0cm　27.0cm　24.0cm　21.0cm

37ページ
鰻さき各種
用途が同じでも地方によってまったく形が異なる庖丁がある。たとえば鰻さきである。左より名古屋の鰻さき、京都の鰻さき、大阪の鰻さき。
名古屋の鰻さき　26.0cm（全長）
京都の鰻さき　22.5cm（全長）
大阪の鰻さき　21.0cm（全長）

38ページ
柳刃刺身庖丁
関西型の刺身庖丁。現在では、この形の刺身庖丁がほとんど全国で使われている。
左より39.0cm　36.0cm　33.0cm　30.0cm　27.0cm　24.0cm　21.0cm　18.0cm

39ページ
フグ引き
フグの刺身用庖丁。
左より36.0cm　30.0cm　24.0cm

40ページ
蛸引き
関東型の刺身庖丁。
左より39.0cm　33.0cm　27.0cm　24.0cm

61ページ

筋引庖丁

肉の筋をとるのに使う。

左より30.0cm　27.0cm　24.0cm

62・63ページ

牛刀

主として左の二本は肉の塊を切り分けるのに、
つぎの二本は野菜切りに、つぎの三本は肉切りに使う。小型の牛刀（22cm、18cm）は家庭
で使われることが多い。特に右端の庖丁は、
文化庖丁ともよばれ、家庭専用のもの。

左より39.0cm　36.0cm　33.0cm　30.0cm　27.0cm

25.5cm　24.0cm　22.0cm　18.0cm

64ページ

ペティナイフ

左より15.0cm　13.5cm　12.0cm

65ページ

ガラすき（左）と骨すき（中央と右）

肉から骨をはずすのに使う。

左より18.0cm　15.0cm　13.5cm

66ページ

ハム切り

ハムを薄くスライスするのに使う。

左より42.0cm　39.0cm　36.0cm　33.0cm

67ページ

カステラ切り

左より42.0cm 39.0cm 36.0cm 33.0cm 30.0cm

68ページ

特種庖丁各種

左から冷凍用、コマ切り用、スモークサーモ
ン用の庖丁。

左より30.0cm　18.0cm　24.0cm

（注記がない場合、寸法は刃渡りを表わす。）

Shops and Sources

The maker of all the knives in this book except those on pages 13, 15–17, 26, and 27 is:

Masamoto Sō Honten K.K.
1–6–5 Azuma-bashi
Sumida-ku, Tokyo
Tel. (03) 622–6356

The Masamoto company was kind enough to loan their products to be photographed and extended the fullest cooperation at all times. The remaining knives are from the collection of Mr. Yoshio Akioka, the author of the introduction.

Two other companies that produce quality household and professional knives are:

Aritsugu Hamono K.K.
4–13 Tsukiji
Chūō-ku, Tokyo
Tel. (03) 541–6890

Sugimoto Hamono K.K.
4–10 Tsukiji
Chūō-ku, Tokyo
Tel. (03) 541–6980

These addresses and sources of supply are included for the convenience of readers desiring to obtain these objects. Letters and orders should be in Japanese.

資料提供者

正本総本店　東京都墨田区吾妻橋1-65　電03(622)6356
13、15〜17、26、27ページの資料は秋岡芳夫氏提供

DATE DUE

F OC 10'80			
GAYLORD			PRINTED IN U.S.A